Body talk

BODY TALK

Bobbie Kalman

 Crabtree Publishing Company

www.crabtreebooks.com

Created by Bobbie Kalman

**Author and
Editor-in-Chief**
Bobbie Kalman

Reading consultant
Elaine Hurst

Editors
Kathy Middleton
Crystal Sikkens

Design
Bobbie Kalman
Katherine Berti

Photo research
Bobbie Kalman

**Production coordinator
and Prepress technician**
Katherine Berti

Photographs by Shutterstock

Library and Archives Canada Cataloguing in Publication

Kalman, Bobbie, 1947-
    Body talk / Bobbie Kalman.

(My world)
ISBN 978-0-7787-9511-7 (bound).--ISBN 978-0-7787-9536-0 (pbk.)

    1. Body language--Juvenile literature. I. Title. II. Series: My
world (St. Catharines, Ont.)

BF637.N66K34 2011   j153.6'9   C2010-901976-8

Library of Congress Cataloging-in-Publication Data

Kalman, Bobbie.
  Body talk / Bobbie Kalman.
    p. cm. -- (My world)
  ISBN 978-0-7787-9536-0 (pbk. : alk. paper) -- ISBN 978-0-7787-9511-7
(reinforced library binding : alk. paper)
  1. Body language--Juvenile literature. I. Title. II. Series.

  BF637.N66K35 2010
  153.6'9--dc22

                            2010011303

Crabtree Publishing Company

www.crabtreebooks.com   1-800-387-7650

Printed in the USA/032017/CG20170131

**Published in Canada
Crabtree Publishing**
616 Welland Ave.
St. Catharines, Ontario
L2M 5V6

**Published in the United States
Crabtree Publishing**
PMB 59051
350 Fifth Avenue, 59th Floor
New York, New York 10118

**Published in the United Kingdom
Crabtree Publishing**
Maritime House
Basin Road North, Hove
BN41 1WR

**Published in Australia
Crabtree Publishing**
386 Mt. Alexander Rd.
Ascot Vale (Melbourne)
VIC 3032

Words to know

angry
(mad)   bored   confused   excited

happy   sad   sorry   worried
(afraid)

We have feelings.

Happy, **sad**, **afraid**, **angry**, (mad) are some of the ways we feel.

Sometimes we say how we feel.

We say, "I am angry!" or "I feel happy."

Our faces also tell how we feel.
The mouths and eyes of these children
show how they feel.
Which child's face is happy?
Which child's face is sad?
Which one is afraid, and which one is mad?

Did you know that your body
can "say" how you feel?
What are the bodies of these boys saying?
Which parts of their bodies are "talking"?

This boy drew a sad face
and a happy face on his legs.
How does he really feel?
How do you know?

Smiling and laughing
show happy feelings.
Hands high in the air
also show that
someone feels happy.

When you feel
very happy
about something,
you are **excited**!

You open your mouth
and eyes wide.
You spread out
your fingers.
Sometimes
you jump for joy!

9

Your arms and hands
can also show other feelings.
They can tell others that you are angry.
Crossed arms say, "I am angry!"

This girl is holding her hand out.

Is her hand saying "hello" or "stop"?

How do the faces, arms, and hands of these children show that they are **bored**?
How do you show that you are bored?

Faces, arms, and hands can also say, "I am afraid." How do these children show that they are afraid?

Activity

Our bodies also say other things.

Match each picture with this body talk:

1. "I wonder..."
2. "It's great!"
3. "I am **confused**."
4. "I am **worried**!"

5. "I am **sorry**."
6. "I get it!"
7. "It's not good."

(d)

(e)

(f)

(g)

15

Notes for adults

Objectives
- to introduce children to the important non-verbal ways they communicate their feelings
- to assist children in identifying the feelings of others by their facial expressions, postures, and gestures

Before reading *Body talk*
Read *I have feelings* to the children. Tell them to pay attention to the pictures in the book and to think about how they show their own feelings.

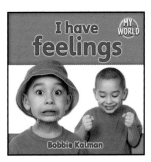

Guided Reading: C

Next, ask the children to read *Body talk*. How do the children in this book communicate their feelings through facial expressions and different body postures?

Reading "body talk"
Read the following story to the class. Pause after each "body talk" clue and ask the children which emotions are being expressed.

Madison's new home
Madison is moving to a new home. She **cries** as she waves goodbye to her friends. When she and her family reach their new apartment building, Madison notices a beautiful playground. She gets out of the car and **jumps up and down, with her arms high in the air**. At the front door of the building, a girl with **crossed arms is tapping her foot**. She is **frowning**. She says to Madison, "My friend promised to come and play with me." Madison **smiles** and says, "I will play with you." The two girls run to the playground together, **laughing**.

Help with Asperger's syndrome
This book can be a big help to children who have Asperger's syndrome. Children with this syndrome may not pick up on social cues and may lack inborn social skills, such as being able to read the body language of others. They may have unusual facial expressions or postures. *I have feelings* and *Body talk* can both be used to familiarize these children with how people show their feelings. From the book, children can also learn how to practice using body language to show their feelings to others. The whole class can play "body-talk charades" and guess the feelings that the children are showing.

For teacher's guide, go to www.crabtreebooks.com/teachersguides